Katherine of Aragon:
A Collection of Poems

by

Alice-Catherine Jennings

Finishing Line Press
Georgetown, Kentucky

Katherine of Aragon:
A Collection of Poems

ACKNOWLEDGMENTS

Grateful acknowledgement is made to the editors of the following journals in
which these poems first appeared under different titles and in slightly different
forms.

The Fertile Source: "Katherine's Prayer," "Katherine" (9)
2013 Round Top Poetry Anthology: "Katherine" (16)

Publisher: Leah Maines

Editor: Christen Kincaid

Cover Art: John Mark Jennings

Author Photo: John Mark Jennings

Cover Design: Elizabeth Maines

Printed in the USA on acid-free paper.
Order online: www.finishinglinepress.com
              also available on amazon.com

Author inquiries and mail orders:
Finishing Line Press
P. O. Box 1626
Georgetown, Kentucky 40324
U. S. A.

Table of Contents

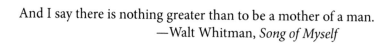

And I say there is nothing greater than to be a mother of a man.
—Walt Whitman, *Song of Myself*

Preface

Katherine of Aragon is a collection of poems set in 16th century England. It begins with the wedding of Katherine of Aragon to King Henry VIII and ends with Katherine's death. The narrative arc of this book is based on actual facts although the content of the poems is a mixture of truth, myth, and imagination commingled with and inspired by the texts of other poets and writers.

You must produce
10.11.1537

cast of characters:

you: *{unknown}woman*
    {every}

speaker: *jane seymour, 3rd wife of henry viii* ——>*roster of emotions*
                                        pride
                                        elation
                                        crosspatch
                                        woe
chorus:

  katherine of aragon, 1st wife of henry viii
  anne boleyn, 2nd wife of henry viii
  the royal midwife

setting: *lying-in room*

                            selected bibliography:
                            story of eve, the bible
                            bestiario, arreola
                            aching for beauty, wang

props: *rosary*
         clear rushes
         arrow, if needed

action:

chorus: *squat.*
        open {cupboards}
            {drawers}
            {chests}

jane: *{emotions deleted}*

you: *(whispers to self) shoot the arrow, for god's sake!*

the end: *{known}*
        {repeat again}

After "You can't deny it" by Evie Shockley
        The New Black. Weslayan University Press, 2011.

bestiario is a reference to *Bestiario* by Juan Jose Arreola, Mortiz,
        2013.

aching for beauty is a reference to *Aching for Beauty: Footbinding
        in China* by Wang Ping, Anchor, 2002.

Katherine~

Love that liveth and reineth in my thought,
that built your seat within my captive breast.
For years your thighs with reddish hairs I sought
with lust that liveth in my thought.
My fingers caressed rosary beads for naught
as each night my naked body I caressed.
Your manhood reineth in my carnal thoughts
and built your seat within my widow's breast.

Love that liveth and reineth in my thought,
That built his seat within my captive breast.
> (From "love that liveth and reigneth in my thought"
> by Henry Howard, Earl of Surrey)

Katherine Announces Her Pregnancy to Henry
08.15.1510

And the sun will dance on my leaves,
and I shall be strong and beautiful...
Sparkles from the ruby aigrette weave
gold glints that dance in the folds of fine hair.
Falling to her hips, long, it caresses the sleeves
of her mousseline de soie robe. She leans
towards the King with a whisper: *I wish*
tagine and tangerines for supper.
His face flushes the future and the sun
will dance on the Queen and she shall be
strong and beautiful through all the seasons.

...and the sun will dance on my leaves, and I shall be strong and
beautiful through all the seasons.
(From "The Pomegranate" by Kahlil Gibran)

The Death of Prince Henry
02.22.1511

frost-shorn pool, lost
among rows of phlox, offshoots
of thorns-moonwort hooks on protons
dolor

Katherine~

> *There are few women who could compete with the queen in*
> *her prime.*
> —Sir Thomas More

I

Victors rising high above, coursing power,
vanquished blunted and muttering in rage
while Thou art gone, I do not cower.
Victors rising high above, coursing power,
ride north did I with regal glower.
To thee I send the bloody coat of James.
Victors rising high above, coursing power,
the vanquished Scots are muttering in rage.

II

Time, time is the house,
and to welcome you I'll string
garlands of eggshells
and rubies. Rush now
to me before the air of winter
dreich ends the capercaillie's
call. Pulse through stone and thick
with your peafowl train erect
while I string garlands of
eggshells and rubies.

victors rising high above, coursing power,
vanquished blunted and muttering in rage
> (From "South Mountain" by Han Yu as translated by
> David Hinton *Classical Chinese Poetry An Anthology,*
> Straus and Giroux, 2008.)

Time, time was the house, and to welcome you
I strung garlands of eggshells and rubies.
> (From "The Welcoming" by Beth Ann Fe___lly,
> *Unmentionables: Poems,* W.W. Norton & Co., 2008)

The Birth of Princess Mary
02.18.1516

Joy
oh joy,
flock of loon,
hoot of owl, show off fowl
bonobo fool who howls *coocoo*.
oh joy…

Katherine's Prayer
12.12.1519

failing,
fallow land, my
womb—*barain, aridez*
devoid of fruit, incapable
matriz.

fecund
fertillus seeds,
produce a spawning womb,
sustain abundant growth, a crop,
a son.

Katherine~

crackle fire winter's dawn fire hearth crackle crackle crack the egg
lady madge snap snap logs, back, crackle crackle heat crack the egg,
crack the egg, the pain, the back, crackle crackle heat erase the chill,
crack crack, stuff my quaint, bind my legs lady anne, bind my legs
tight tight stop the crackle stop the heat hold my legs, crack the back,
the pain, the egg, no! no! no! expel the crack, the bones, the nails,
the chinks, crack crack crackle no! no! no! crack crack add the logs,
the rags, chunks of bone crack crack crackle heat cracks brows burn
crackle crackle teeth crack the eggs crack the pain, the heat...
   soaked in sorrow, fearful at the sight,
    for all that, I lay there a long while

I was soaked in sorrow, fearful at the sight
For all that, I lay there a long while.
  (From "The Vision of the Cross" as translated from the
  Anglo-Saxon by Ciara Carson, *The Word Exchange*
  Anglo-Saxon Poems, W.W. Norton & Co., Inc.)

After the Victory at Pavia
03.01.1525

I

Soak a pound of bread, stale,
in milk until plumped. Press
out the moisture with the fingers
of your hands, the hands you use
to lift the salt from the bin,
the hands you use to yank
the celeriac from the ground,
now dank, the ones you use
to slit the liver, still wet,
out of the chicken's breast.

II

We ate special dishes to mark the occasion.
There was Pavia this and Pavia that
and even a dish called Spanish Delight.
The Pavia Peacock was served cold
with chopped jelly and sauce poivrade.

III

They say it's Anne's hair that attracts
him. *Cheveux d'ange*, angel
hair, they call it. There's the lift
at the nape of the neck that gives
rise to the tendrils, curled, cresting
on top. Her Ladies consider this up-
do her aspect most appealing but I'd
opine not. No, it's the slim wisp
of darkness she combs down
from the crafted nest. She slips
it in front of her left ear, letting
it graze near her brow as it topples.
Henry's attention shifts; he stares
into her coal eyes, those devil eyes.

IV
The Queen placed her hand on the King's
wrists. Henry smiled recalling Katherine
at twenty-three and he at eighteen, the
time before:
the stillborn daughter,
the dead son;
the autumn loss;
the spring stillborn, another son;
a third girl birthed dead,
only Mary, alive, before
her monthlies stopped.

Original recipe for "Roast Young Peacock" appeared in *Vintage Gourmet*, December 1951.

We ate special dishes which were given new names to mark the occasion: Pavia Peacock and Pavia Pudding, Spanish Delight and Blanc Mange
(From *The Other Boleyn Girl* by Philippa Gregory, Pocket Books, 2001.)

"Cheveux d'Ange" is a reference to a work by the same name by Laura Lark, temporary exhibition at The Blanton Museum of Art, Austin, Texas. Ink marker on Tyvek, 2003.

Katherine Discovers "The King's Great Matter"
02.02.1527

The Frost performs its secret ministry
unhelped by any wind. The owlet cries
nestled in a hollow, barely visible
like spicules of ice, her indignity
a soft rime. A herald of the night, the oule
digests her ken, Ah bitter chill it was!
as Frost performs its secret ministry
unhelped by any wind—the owlet's cry.

The Frost performs its secret ministry
Unhelped by any wind. The owlet's cry
> (From "After Frost at Midnight" by Samuel Taylor
> Coleridge)

Ah, bitter chill it was!
> (From "The Eve of St. Agnes" by John Keats)

Katherine~

Three in the morning he slithers in through somewhere—
not sure where as even when the night is warm
and the windows are open, the screens are shut tight.
I had them tacked down just in case but like the mice he eats,
a snake can compress his body and edge it through
a space as small as my left nostril while I'm sleeping.

I hardly notice his glide down my throat until
he injects me with his venom. My spleen tightens
causing a pain so fierce, it wakes me up. My mind shakes
with worry. My left hip aches from my body's thrashing.
Get out! I scream as I run down the stairs retching
up its bilious body onto the blood-stained floor.

Katherine Considers the Pope's Request to Enter the Convent
10.24.1528

I

Memories ache on, same as yesterday
and the last winter's moon gone dark.
She lays her head on the hard rail and prays.
Memories ache on and on as yesterday.
The Pope's words sway as a willow weak.
He knows it is our Lord she must obey.
Memories ache on, same as yesterday
and the last winter's moon gone dark.

II

Across this lake, in the turn of a head
mountain greens furl into white cloud.
She daydreams of the eve she wed.
Across the lake, with the turn of her heart
the moment clear when her maidenhead
was rendered to the King. Why doubt
Henry now? Who has turned his head
from mountain greens to dark, dark clouds?

III

Star-mother never mated—so how is it
she gave birth to nine star-children?

IV

When light and dark are still a blur
who can see through to their source.
Because the world around her twirls,
light and dark are still a blur.
The council meets, the people talk. A whirl
of gossip, plots and voices hoarse.
When light and dark are still a blur
who can see through to their source?

Memories ache on, same as yesterday
and the last winter's moon gone dark.
> (From "New Year's" by Wei Ying Wu as translated by
> David Hinton, *Classical Chinese Poetry An Anthology*,
> Straus and Giroux, 2008.)

Across this lake, in the turn of a head
Mountain greens furl into white clouds.
> (From "Vagary Lake" by Wang Wei as translated by
> David Hinton , *Classical Chinese Poetry An Anthology*,
> Straus and Giroux, 2008.)

Star Mother never mated—so how is it
She gave birth to nine star-children?
> (From "The Songs of Ch'u" as translated by David
> Hinton, *Classical Chinese Poetry An Anthology*, Straus
> and Giroux, 2008.)

When light and dark are still a blur
Who can see through to their source
> (From "The Songs of Ch'u" as translated by David
> Hinton, *Classical Chinese Poetry An Anthology*, Straus
> and Giroux, 2008.)

Katherine~

I'll tell you my mirror is blue
and my eyes are blue
and my veins are blue
spiders in my ankles.

I'll tell you my hair is blue
grey like mist at winter's dawn.

I'll tell you my soul is blue
lost in a labyrinth of regret.

I'll tell you my shadow is blue
I know you feel its weight.

I'll tell you my memory is blue
ice, cracked open
and ruined by your infidelity.

I'll tell you my sky is blue
and that before

it was bright.
(This is the harshest blue.)

I'll tell you my fatigue is blue.
It comes in insensate blocks

without start or finish.

And finally that I see blue,
only blue.

After "Red or Nothing" by Andre Velter, as translated by Marilyn Hacker, *New European Poets*, Gray Wolf Press, 2008

Will Somers, the King's Fool~

The door of the house at Christmastime
I…wonder what happened to that lady.
Let the bells this morning chime!
The tables at court at Christmastime,
full of wassail, saffron, meat stuffed pies.
Fatten cheer and stay the light that's fading
upon the winter greens at Christmastime.
I…wonder what happened to that lady.

The door of the house at Christmastime,
I'll always wonder what happened to that lady.
> (From *Working from Memory* by William Christenberry,
> Steidel, 2008.)

Katherine in Exile
12.25.1531

Hair tossed and tumbled to one side, she braves dawn cold.
Candles crying red tears resent dawn light filling the sky
on this sacred day, when loss has been foretold.
Hair tossed and tumbled to one side, she braves dawn cold.
She circles the yard and tightens the ruff around her neck.
Her cook prepares the candied apples, warms the Rhenish wines.
The King's love tumbles to another's side while she braves dawn cold.
Candles crying red tears resent dawn light filling the sky.

Hair tossed and tumbled to one side, she braves dawn cold
Candles crying red tears resent dawn light filling the sky
> (From "Swallow Terrace" by Li Shang-Yin as translated by
> David Hinton, *Classical Chinese Poetry An Anthology*,
> Straus and Giroux, 2008.)

Katherine~

> *In this world I will confess myself to be the king's true wife, and*
> *in the next they will know how unreasonably I am afflicted.*
> —*Katherine of Aragon*

There is not one false stitch;
all is so neat and true.
Even knots on the stretched
pale cloth—not one false stitch.
I draw through the fabric
the threads, emerald and azul.
There is not one false stitch;
I am the Queen so true.

There was not one false stitch ...;
all was so neat and true
> (From "The Elves and the Shoemaker" by the Brothers
> Grimm)

The Death of Katherine of Aragon
01.07.1536

Wrap me she said *in my caftan, the one
the color of Granada, a watermelon-blush.*

Her ladies bathed her with oven-warmed rags
scented with spices of Catalan crème, slipped

the silk garment over her head, draping
the folds upon edges of ribs, hips and legs.

Yet, a false weft it was as the cloth could
not veil years spun on a moist foreign land,

nor cure the dampness that swelled her ankles
and blackened her *sangre*-blue wrists.

After "The Death of Rachel" by Antonio Carneo, oil on canvas
circa 1660-70, Blanton Museum of Art, Austin, Texas

A Chronology of Katherine of Aragon

1485: Katherine is born to King Ferdinand II and Queen Isabella I of Spain.

1501: Katherine marries Prince Arthur, the heir to the English throne.

1502: Prince Arthur dies.

1509: Katherine marries King Henry VIII, Prince Arthur's younger brother. A few weeks later, she is crowned Queen of England.

1510: Katherine has a stillborn daughter.

1511: Katherine has a son, Henry, Duke of Cornwell. He lives 52 days.

1513: The Scots invade England. Katherine rides north in full army to address the English troops. King James IV of Scotland is killed in the Battle of Flodden. A few months later, Katherine has a son who is either stillborn or lives for a few hours.

1514: Another son is born. He lives for a few hours.

1516: A daughter, Mary, is born. She survives eventually becoming Mary, Queen of England.

1518: A daughter is born. She lives for seven days.

1525: Henry VIII becomes infatuated with Anne Boleyn, a lady-in-waiting to Katherine.

1527: Henry VIII asks the Catholic Church to invalidate his marriage to Katherine. The Pope stalls. Henry's desire to end his marriage to Katherine becomes known as "The King's Great Matter."

1531/1532: Katherine is exiled.

1533: Henry VIII secretly marries Anne Boleyn and later that same year crowns her Queen of England.

1536: Katherine dies in exile at Kimbolton Castle.

Alice-Catherine Jennings holds an MA in Slavic Languages and Literatures from The University of Texas at Austin and an MFA in Writing from Spalding University. Her poetry has appeared in various publications including *Hawai'i Review, Penumbra, The Louisville Review, Boyne Berries, GTK Creative, The Poets' Republic,* and *First Literary Review East.*